Follow Me Around™
China

By Wiley Blevins

SCHOLASTIC

Content Consultant: Zhiqun Zhu, PhD, Professor of Political Science and International Relations and Director of the China Institute, Bucknell University, Lewisburg, Pennsylvania

Library of Congress Cataloging-in-Publication Data
Names: Blevins, Wiley, author.
Title: China / by Wiley Blevins.
Description: New York : Children's Press, Scholastic, 2018. | Series: Follow me around | Includes bibliographical references and index.
Identifiers: LCCN 2016049402| ISBN 9780531237076 (library binding) | ISBN9780531239735 (pbk.)
Subjects: LCSH: China—Juvenile literature.
Classification: LCC DS706 .B555 2018 | DDC 951—dc23
LC record available at https://lccn.loc.gov/2016049402

Design: Judith Christ Lafond & Anna Tunick Tabachnik
Text: Wiley Blevins
© 2018 Scholastic Inc.

1 2 3 4 5 6 7 8 9 10 R 27 26 25 24 23 22 21 20 19 18

Photos ©: cover background: CSP_SeanPavonePhoto/age fotostock; cover child: Linqong/Dreamstime; back cover: Linqong/Dreamstime; 1: Linqong/Dreamstime; 3 bottom right: blue jean images/Getty Images; 3 background: Public Domain; 4 left: Linqong/Dreamstime; 6 left: XiXinXing/Getty Images; 6 right: Copyright by Ata Mohammad Adnan/Getty Images; 7: Eastphoto/age fotostock; 8: Yann Layma/Getty Images; 9 top: pidjoe/iStockphoto; 9 bottom: Y_L/Shutterstock; 10 top: Wolfgang Kaehler/LightRocket/Getty Images; 10 bottom: MrsWilkins/iStockphoto; 11 left: Futaba Hayashi/Dreamstime; 11 right: Wang HE/Getty Images; 12-13 background: Vadim Yerofeyev/Dreamstime; 12 right: KC Hunter/Alamy Images; 12-13 cartoons: Tomacco/iStockphoto; 14 top: Vitalyedush/Dreamstime; 14 bottom: Lou Linwei/Alamy Images; 15 left: Hufton and Crow/Getty Images; 15 right: Sofiaworld/Dreamstime; 16 top: Kok Kai Ng/Getty Images; 16 bottom: cyoginan/Thinkstock; 17 left: aphotostory/Shutterstock; 17 center: LatitudeStock - Mel Longhurst/Getty Images; 17 top right: craftvision/iStockphoto; 17 bottom right: Nikada/iStockphoto; 18 top: Jonathan Irish/Getty Images; 18 bottom left: North Wind Picture Archives/Alamy Images; 18 bottom right: Emma Gawen/Getty Images; 19 top: DuKai photographer/Getty Images; 19 bottom left: Mongolia/China: A Mongol horseman with a composite bow, c. 13th century/Pictures from History/Bridgeman Art Library; 19 bottom center: ullstein bild/The Granger Collection; 19 bottom right: Apic/Getty Images; 20 top umbrella: Homydesign/Dreamstime; 20 top fireworks: WIN-Initiative/Neleman/Getty Images; 20 top toilet paper: lukethelake/Shutterstock; 20 bottom: Pete Oxford/Minden Pictures; 21 top left mask: Terry Allen/Alamy Images; 21 top right mask: VCG/Getty Images; 21 bottom right mask: swisshippo/iStockphoto; 21 bottom left: Marilyn Barbone/Dreamstime; 21 bottom center: Maocheng/Dreamstime; 22 top: Feng Li/Getty Images; 22 bottom: CSP_homestudio/age fotostock; 23 top left: Toa55/Shutterstock; 23 center left top: Canghia76/Dreamstime; 23 center left bottom: VCG/Getty Images; 23 bottom left: SEUX Paula/age fotostock; 23 right: szefei/iStockphoto; 24 top: chinaphotographer/iStockphoto; 24 center: cienpies/iStockphoto; 24 bottom: popovaphoto/iStockphoto; 25 top left: David Silverman/Getty Images; 25 top center: Dirck Halstead/Getty Images; 25 bottom left: Tony Duffy/Getty Images; 25 bottom right: Herve Bruhat/Getty Images; 25 top right: blue jean images/Getty Images; 26 bottom: Norman Chan/Dreamstime; 26 top right: Mark Mawson/robertharding/Getty Images; 27 top left: Phiseksit/Dreamstime; 27 center: Kerrick/iStockphoto; 27 top right: GlobalP/iStockphoto; 27 bottom left: CPA Media - Pictures from History/The Granger Collection; 27 bottom right: China Photos/Getty Images; 28 D: VCG/Getty Images; 28 E: yangchao/iStockphoto; 28 B: Chu Yong/Getty Images; 28 A: Howie Garber/age fotostock; 28 G: Victor Korchenko/age fotostock; 28 F: VCG/Getty Images; 28 C: Tony Waltham/age fotostock; 29 left: anants/iStockphoto; 29 right: anants/iStockphoto; 30 top right: camelt/iStockphoto; 30 top left: marigold_88/iStockphoto; 30 bottom: Linqong/Dreamstime; Maps by Jim McMahon.

Table of Contents

Where in the World Is China?.. 4

Home Sweet Home.. 6

Food We Eat 8

Let's Go to School.. 10

The Legend of Mulan 12

Around My Big Country.. 14

Our Fascinating History 18

Great Things from China 20

Celebrate!.. 22

Time to Play... 24

You Won't Believe This!........................... 26

Guessing Game!..................................... 28

How to Prepare for Your Visit 29

The United States Compared to China 30

Glossary 31

Index... 32

Where in the World Is China?

Nǐ hǎo (nee how) from China! That's how we say "Hello." I'm Wàng, your tour guide. My name means "hope" or "wish." It is my hope that someday you'll get to visit my big and fascinating country.

China is located in Asia. Many people say that China is shaped like a rooster facing east. Take a look. You can almost see a feathery head and pointy beak.

About one-fifth of all the world's people live in China. That's 1.4 billion people. Talk about crowded! Half of the people in China live in the countryside. The other half live in our many large cities. Come on, let me show you around.

Fast Facts:

- Zhōngguó (jung-gwah), meaning "middle kingdom," is the name of China in **Mandarin** Chinese. Mandarin is the most common group of languages spoken in China.

- China stretches more than 3,000 miles (4,828 kilometers) from east to west.

- Most people live on the east coast or near two big rivers: the Yangtze (meaning "long river") and the Yellow Rivers.

- The north is covered in deserts (the Gobi and the Taklamakan).

- The west has many mountains (such as Mount Everest).

- More than 90 percent of the people are Han Chinese.

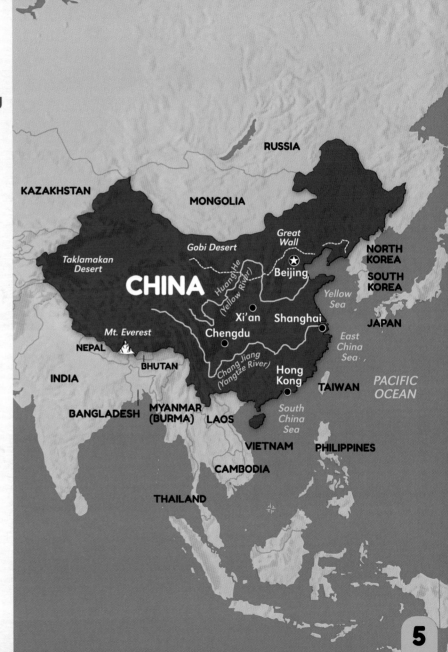

RUSSIA

KAZAKHSTAN

MONGOLIA

Great Wall

Gobi Desert

Taklamakan Desert

CHINA

Huang He (Yellow River)

Beijing

NORTH KOREA

SOUTH KOREA

Yellow Sea

Xi'an

Shanghai

JAPAN

Chengdu

East China Sea

Mt. Everest

NEPAL

BHUTAN

Chang Jiang (Yangtze River)

Hong Kong

PACIFIC OCEAN

INDIA

TAIWAN

BANGLADESH

MYANMAR (BURMA)

LAOS

South China Sea

VIETNAM

PHILIPPINES

CAMBODIA

THAILAND

Many families have three or more generations living together.

Shoes and slippers can be stored in a special place by the door.

Home Sweet Home

I am from Beijing, China. I live with my parents and grandparents in our small apartment. It's common in China to live with family members from many generations. I'm an only child, which is also common, especially in the cities. For a long time, the law limited families to one child each. But that's starting to change. My family name is Li.

In China, we say our family name first. So, my official name is Li Wàng. It's like you saying Smith Jack instead of Jack Smith. But you can call me Wàng.

If you visit my home, the first thing you need to do is take off your shoes. We usually do not wear shoes indoors. Instead, we put on slippers.

My bedroom is not much different from many in the United States.

We decorate using *fĕng shuĭ* (fung shway). It is our way of living in harmony with our surroundings. Fĕng shuĭ, which means "wind and water," determines how we arrange our furniture, the colors and fabrics we use, and where we put plants. We believe that good fĕng shuĭ in a home brings health, happiness, and success.

How to Make a Fĕng shuĭ Bedroom

These four rules are the secret to a calm and peaceful bedroom.

1 **Be careful** that the head of your bed is not under a window.

2 **Place the bed** so you can look out the window, but make sure you don't face the door when you are in bed.

3 **Avoid any clutter.** (Your parents will like that rule!)

4 **Never use** bright colors on the walls or sheets. It's hard to relax.

A family digs in with their chopsticks.

Food We Eat

China is a huge country. I mean really big! Like other big countries, each **region** has its own special food, from spicy to mild. Some common dishes you might enjoy here are sticky rice, slurpy noodles, a wide range of teas, soup, dumplings, lots of pork, and stir-fry.

We usually eat meals with our whole family. The food is served in large dishes, which we share. Even in a restaurant, you won't order a plate just for you. Instead, someone will order lots of plates of steaming, yummy food for everyone to dig into.

When not at home, you can grab a bite on one of our Snack Streets. Buy a dumpling or a sweet treat. Here you'll also find lots of creepy-crawly food on a stick. You can get scorpions, spiders, and loads of roasted insects. Yum!

Forget about forks and knives when eating in China. We eat with chopsticks. You might want to practice before you come. Here's how:

1 Place the thick end of a chopstick in the crook of your thumb.

2 Let the thin end rest on your ring finger.

3 Place the other chopstick between the tips of your first two fingers and the tip of your thumb.

4 To grab food, move the top chopstick up and down.

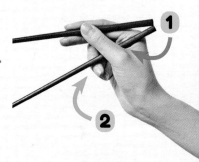

Eating Etiquette

When using **chopsticks, do not point them at someone**. Also, do not place them across the top of your bowl when you're finished. That's just rude!

Remember, it's okay to hold a soup or rice bowl up to your mouth. But **never cut your noodles**. We think that means you'll have a short life.

And don't forget to **compliment the cook**. A simple xie-xie (sheh-sheh), or thank you, will do.

Lastly, **always leave a little food on your plate**. If not, your dinner host will think you're leaving hungry. Not good!

Let's Go to School

In China, we start school at age six. We have to study hard because at age 18, we take a challenging two-day test. It's called the Gāokao. This test determines who can go to college. We study hundreds of hours for it.

Most of our school lessons are taught in Standard Mandarin. That's the official language in China. We also study English as a second language. You might be surprised when you visit our classrooms. Some have 50 to 60 students crammed into one room. But I'm lucky. I get to sit next to my best péngyou (pung-yoh), or friend.

One of the first things we learn in school is how to read and write Chinese characters. These are pictures that stand for words. We use these characters instead of letters. We must learn about 2,500 characters to read and write simple books and stories.

友
friend

It is important to know how to count to 10 when you visit China.

一	1	**yī** *(yee)*
二	2	**èr** *(ar)*
三	3	**sān** *(sun)*
四	4	**sì** *(suh)*
五	5	**wǔ** *(woo)*
六	6	**liù** *(lee-oh)*
七	7	**qī** *(chee)*
八	8	**bā** *(bah)*
九	9	**jiǔ** *(chee-oh)*
十	10	**shí** *(shuh)*

A typical lunch at my school has lots of healthy and tasty foods.

The Legend of Mulan

In school we read a lot of folktales and <u>legends</u> from long ago. One of my favorites is the story of Mulan.

Long ago there lived a girl named Mulan. Her father had been a strong and powerful general, but now he was sick and weak with age. Mulan's father was different from most fathers. He taught Mulan how to ride a horse. He also taught her how to use weapons. These were things girls usually didn't learn.

One day soldiers rode into town. War was coming!

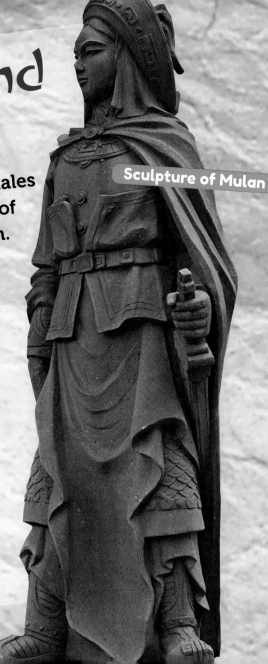

Sculpture of Mulan

They needed men to fight the Mongols, invaders from Mongolia to the northwest. The soldiers posted a list of the men they needed. Mulan's father's name was on it. Fearful for his life, Mulan stole her father's armor, dressed like a male soldier, and took his place.

Years passed, and the war raged on. Mulan fought bravely, but she was always careful that no one discovered she was a girl. Mulan won many awards for her courage. At the end of the war, the **emperor** gave her a special horse and a bagful of money. Mulan raced back home. She wanted to return to a quiet life with her father.

One day, some fellow soldiers stopped by her home. When they found out Mulan was a girl, they couldn't believe their eyes. They spread her story throughout China. Mulan, the girl who saved her father's life. The girl who helped save China.

Forbidden City

Around My Big Country

Beijing: Capital City

Welcome to my city, Beijing. It's the capital of China. When you visit, you'll want to go first to Tiananmen Square. It's a popular gathering place and the gateway to the Forbidden City—the most famous tourist spot in Beijing.

The Forbidden City was built long ago during the Ming **dynasty**. It served as the home of the emperor. It had 980 buildings and nine throne rooms. Commoners like you and me were forbidden from entering it. That's how it got its name. If you got caught sneaking in or out, you would be killed. Yikes!

The other famous thing you'll see in Beijing, unfortunately, is pollution. With over 14 million people and tons of cars and factories billowing smoke, this is a real problem. That's why you'll spot many people wearing masks. They look like a doctor's surgical mask. Most people wear them when walking around or riding their bikes. You might want to bring one, too.

Galaxy SOHO by Zaha Hadid

Great Wall of China

The Great Wall

A short ride from Beijing, you can explore part of the Great Wall. This wall was started over 2,000 years ago and stretches about 5,300 miles (8,500 km). Chinese emperors built it to keep out invaders.

It takes about an hour to hike to the top of the wall. But you should give it a try, if you're able. The view is amazing. If you're tired from the hike, don't worry. Today you can hop on a slide that takes you all the way down. Wheee!

Shanghai skyline

Maglev train

Shanghai: Large and Modern

Although Beijing is the capital city, Shanghai is our biggest. More than 23 million people live there, and you can find some of the coolest modern buildings in the world.

You can quickly zip to the Pudong International Airport using the Shanghai Maglev train. Hang on to your hats! This train can go as fast as 268 miles (431 km) per hour. That's the fastest train on earth. But even more remarkable is that this train has no wheels. Líng! Zero! The train hovers above the runway using powerful magnets. It's as though the train is floating in air.

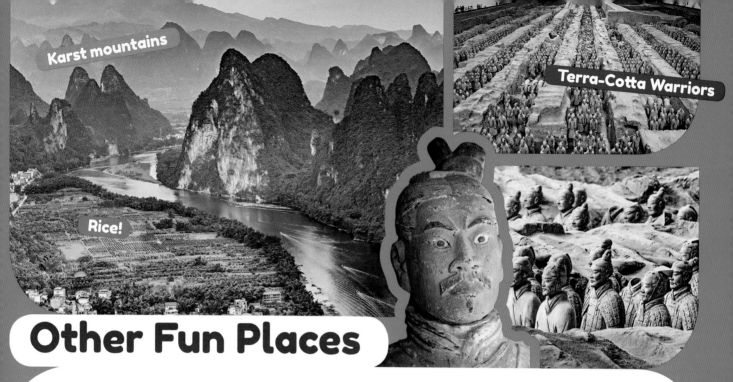

Karst mountains

Rice!

Terra-Cotta Warriors

Other Fun Places

Travel west to Xi'an to see one of the world's greatest **archaeological** finds: the Terra-Cotta Warriors. You'll be amazed. These life-size clay figures were made to guard the grave of Qin Shi Huang, the first emperor of China, 2,200 years ago. In addition to the more than 8,000 warriors, you'll see horses, chariots, acrobats, and musicians.

For another out-of-this-world adventure, take a boat ride along the Li River in the south. This trip will take you past karst mountain formations. You'll find these strange but stunning mountains between the cities of Guilin and Yangshuo. Surrounding them are beautiful terraced fields. This is where farmers grow our most important crop in China—rice!

Our Fascinating History

Rickshaw

We're proud of our country's 4,000-year history. But you don't need to read a book to learn about our past. You can catch a glimpse of it by visiting a hútong, or **traditional** neighborhood. These old-time neighborhoods can be found in Beijing and other cities. My favorite way to travel the narrow, winding streets of a hútong is by riding on a rickshaw. Hop on and enjoy!

Silk Road

Buddha

Timeline: China's Ruling Dynasties

2070–221 BCE
Xia, Shang, Zhou
Earliest peoples live along the Yellow River. Planting and irrigating rice begins.

221–207 BCE
Qin
China is first united. The Great Wall is started.

207 BCE–220 CE
Han
The Silk Road, the major trade route in the region, is started. Paper is invented.

581–618
Sui
Buddhism, one of the main religions in China, develops. The Grand Canal is started.

618–907
Tang
Printed books first become available.

220–589
(China not unified)

Hútong

Mongols attack!

Pu Yi

Mao

960–1279

Song
Gunpowder is first developed by the Chinese. The wok is also invented.

907–960
(China not unified)

1279–1368

Yuan
The Mongols take over China. Many Muslims move to China.

1368–1644

Ming
The Forbidden City is built. Admiral Zheng He's voyages explore the seas.

1644–1912

Qing
China expands. The last emperor, Pu Yi, rules.

1912–today

Modern Era
Revolutionaries establish Asia's first republic. Mao Zedong's Communist Party takes over in 1949.

Great Things from China

Throughout China's history, our people have given the world many important inventions. We're really proud of this! These inventions include yo-yos, umbrellas, sheets of paper, noodles, fireworks, paper money, playing cards, bristle toothbrushes, restaurant menus, tea, and toilet paper. Let's all thank China for that last one!

China is home to the cuddliest animal on the planet and my mom's favorite: the giant panda. If you want to see one gnawing on a piece of bamboo, go to Chengdu in south-western China. We went there on a family trip once. These pandas are considered a national treasure. Though once **endangered**, their population has grown, thanks to our efforts to save them!

The Chinese Opera is a traditional art form. The actors wear colorful, sometimes scary, masks. Each mask represents a different emotion. These operas express tales from long ago and retell important events from our history. The shows are a must-see for visitors, and my family goes every year.

生日快樂

Happy Birthday

Calligraphy is another popular art form. You use special brushes and black ink or paint. Try it! Make a calligraphy birthday card for someone using these Chinese characters.

Celebrate!

Everyone loves a holiday, and we have some fun ones in China. Chinese New Year is the biggest and most popular. It is also called the Spring **Festival**. I love this time of year because the celebration lasts for 15 days! People travel long distances to be with their families. Most businesses close. Many people get haircuts and new clothes to start the year. Dragons, red envelopes filled with money, fireworks, tangerines and oranges for luck, and dancing lions are common sights.

February

Lantern Festival
Marks the end of the Chinese New Year festivities. Children solve riddles on the lanterns.

April

Qing Ming Festival
This spring festival is held to remember one's **ancestors**. Their graves are swept clean, and flowers or fruit are put on them.

June

Dragon Boat Festival
Teams race down the river in colorful dragon boats. The holiday honors Qu Yuan, an honest and wise poet in ancient China.

September

Moon Festival
Celebrates the autumn harvest and family. Special mooncakes are made.

Make Mooncakes

You Will Need:
- 1 tube of **crescent dinner roll dough**
- ½ cup **jam** (strawberry or raspberry)
- 1 tablespoon melted **butter**

Ask a trusted adult for help.

1 **Preheat** the oven to the temperature on the crescent roll dough tube.

2 **Unroll** each crescent roll to form a triangle.

3 **Put a teaspoon** of jam in the center of each triangle.

4 **Roll up the dough** to close over the jam. **Turn the mooncakes** so that the smooth side is on top.

5 **Brush** melted butter on top and **bake** them for the time listed in the directions.

Let the mooncakes cool for 20 minutes. Then pop them into your mouth and enjoy!

Dragon kite!

Time to Play

Kids in China love kites. These flying toys come in many colors and shapes. I have one shaped like a dragon. Along with butterflies, these are the most popular kites. But you can also find kites in the shape of frogs, tigers, goldfish, characters from legends, and many other designs.

Chinese checkers and mah-jongg are very popular board games for kids of all ages, young and old. My favorite game to play with friends is Jiànzi. It is also known as Chinese shuttlecock or Hacky Sack. Use your feet, knees, or head to hold the shuttlecock—just don't let it drop!

Tangrams are also popular: seven differently shaped pieces are made out of a square of paper or wood. You can make many things—animals, people, boats, buildings—by arranging the shapes in different ways. Give it a try!

Tangrams

Tai chi

Kung fu

Shuttlecock

Gymnastics

Ping-Pong

Sports are a popular pastime in China. Ping-Pong, basketball, badminton, soccer, and gymnastics are favorites. But you don't have to join a team to have fun. Go to a park in the morning and you'll see lots of people doing tai chi *(tye chee)*. This is an exercise using slow, relaxing movements. My grandparents do it every morning. It's a great way to stay healthy and calm.

Kung fu *(kung foo)* is also popular. It is an ancient martial art, or way of fighting. It involves quick, strong kicks and is featured in many of our movies. Kick! Pow! Spin!

You Won't Believe This!

The number 8 is lucky. The Mandarin word for "eight" sounds like the word for "prosperous." The 2008 Summer Olympics in Beijing, China, started on August 8 (8/8/2008) at 8:08 p.m.

8

Goldfish are a symbol of wealth.

The number 4 is unlucky to us because the word for "four" (sì) sounds like the word for "death."

4

Dragons are everywhere in China—in art, parades, legends, and more. A dragon, of course, is a made-up animal. But I wish it were real!

A dragon has a camel's head, a deer's antlers, a lobster's eyes, an ox's ears, a goat's beard, an eagle's claws, a snake's body, and a frog's belly, and is covered with fish scales.

Red is the color for luck and is worn on holidays. It is also the color of happiness.

Chirp! Chirp! Cats and dogs are common pets around the world. But many kids in China also have pet crickets. We keep them in small cages. Birds and large goldfish are popular, too.

Mandarin words have different meanings based on how they are said. For example, ma can mean "mother" or "horse" depending on your tone (the rise or fall of your voice). So be careful what you call your mom! She might "neigh" when she answers.

Long ago, small feet were a sign of beauty. It was common to bind feet so that they did not grow. Many adult women had the foot size of a three- to five-year-old child. Most could not walk as a result. Ouch!

Long ago, only royalty, such as emperors, could wear the color yellow. People could be thrown in jail (or worse) if they wore it. Uh-oh!

Guessing Game!

Here are some other great sites around China. Can you guess their names?

Blast off to space from here!

D

1. Shilin Stone Forest
2. Dazu Rock Carvings
3. Jiuquan Space Center
4. Three Gorges Dam
5. Mid-Air Temple in Datong, Shanxi
6. Dragon's Backbone Rice Terraces
7. Victoria Harbor in Hong Kong

This temple looks like it's magically floating in the air.
B

E

These sculptures were carved long ago in the sides of hills.

Lots of China's rice grows on these fields, carved into the sides of hills like stair steps.
A

This looks like a forest of stone trees.
C

F

This popular place for a boat ride is in a well-known territory of China.
G

This is the world's largest power station, using the water of the Yangtze River.

How to Prepare for Your Visit

By now, you should be ready to hop on a plane to China. Here are some tips to prepare for your trip.

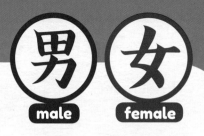

male · female

① Before you come to China, exchange your money. Our money is called **renminbi** (RMB for short) or **yuan**. You'll need it to buy fun souvenirs.

② Bring a **converter** for your electronics. Otherwise, your smartphone's charger won't be able to fit into the outlet!

③ Bring **medicines** (especially for your stomach). If you become sick, don't be surprised if the doctor sticks needles all over your body. This is called **acupuncture**, and it doesn't hurt. Honest! The needles are very skinny, much skinnier than a needle nurses use to give you shots. Acupuncture helps the body heal itself. This and some herbs will soon have you feeling better.

④ Write down the **signs** for **male (men)** and **female (women)** in Chinese characters. You'll need them to find the right bathroom . . . and fast. If you forget, remember that the men's room is usually on the left and the women's is on the right. Don't be surprised if you get a "squatty-potty" instead of what you're used to at home. And don't forget to **grab the toilet paper BEFORE you enter**. It can sometimes be purchased right outside the bathroom. Better yet, carry your own roll! Most public bathrooms do not have toilet paper.

⑤ Buy lots of **bottled water** when you arrive. Never drink water from a faucet or tap. When you're in a new country, drinking the tap water there might make you sick.

29

The United States Compared to China

	United States of America (USA)	People's Republic of China (PRC)
Official Name	United States of America (USA)	People's Republic of China (PRC)
Official Language	No official language, though English is most commonly used	Mandarin (the most common of 8 main Chinese dialects; Cantonese comes next)
Population	325 million	1.4 billion
Common Words	yes, no, please	shì, bùshì, qǐng
Flag		
Money	Dollar	Renminbi (RMB) or yuan
Location	North America	Eastern Asia
Highest Point	Mount McKinley	Mount Everest
Lowest Point	Death Valley	Turpan Pendi
National Anthem	"The Star-Spangled Banner"	"The March of the Volunteers"

So now you know some important and fascinating things about my country, China. I hope to see you someday exploring one of our bustling cities, riding a boat down one of our winding rivers, or standing in awe at one of our famous sights. Until then . . . zài-jiàn (zigh-jee-en)! Good-bye!

Glossary

acupuncture
(AK-yoo-pungk-chur)
a way of treating illness or pain by sticking needles in different parts of the body

---

ancestors
(AN-ses-turz)
members of a family who lived long ago

---

archaeological
(ahr-kee-ah-LAH-ji-kuhl)
related to the study of the distant past, which often involves digging up old buildings, objects, and bones and examining them carefully

---

calligraphy
(kuh-LIG-ruh-fee)
decorative handwriting

---

dynasty
(DYE-nuh-stee)
a series of rulers belonging to the same family

---

emperor *(EM-pur-ur)*
the ruler of an empire

---

endangered
(en-DAYN-jurd)
a plant or animal that is in danger of becoming extinct, or dying out

---

festival *(FES-tuh-vuhl)*
a celebration or holiday

legends *(LEJ-uhndz)*
stories handed down from earlier times that are often based on fact, though not entirely true

---

Mandarin *(MAN-duh-rin)*
the main dialect, or form of language, spoken in China

---

region *(REE-juhn)*
a general area or a specific district or territory

---

traditional
(truh-DISH-uhn-uhl)
related to the customs, ideas, and beliefs that are handed down from one generation to the next

Index

animals, 17, 20, 24, 26, 27
art, 21, 26, 28
cities, 14, 16, 17, 18, 26
food, 8–9, 17, 23
games, 24, 25

Great Wall, 15, 18
history, 15, 17, 18–19, 20, 23
holidays, 22–23
homes, 6–7, 14

land, 4–5, 17, 30
language, 4, 10-11, 27, 29
money, 20, 22, 29, 30
Mulan, 12–13
school, 10, 12

Facts for Now

Visit this Scholastic website for more information on China and to download the Teaching Guide for this series:

www.factsfornow.scholastic.com   Enter the keyword **CHINA**

About the Author

Wiley Blevins lives and works in New York City. His greatest love is traveling, and he has been to China many times. He has also written several books for children in China, including books about popular TV characters there such as Bodhi and Friends, Little Twin Stars, and My Melody.